Layered
Soup
Mixes
in Jars
Original Recipes For Gift Giving
Jackie Gannaway

Published in Austin, TX by COOKBOOK CUPBOARD,
P.O. Box 50053, Austin, TX 78763
(512) 477-7070 phone (512) 891-0094 fax

ISBN 0-885597-27-4

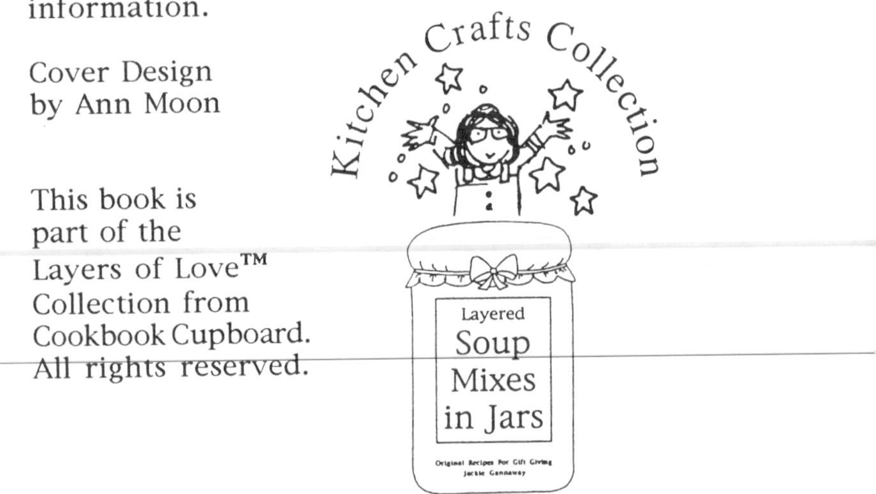

Cover Design
by Ann Moon

This book is part of the Layers of Love™ Collection from Cookbook Cupboard.

Mail Order Information

To order a copy of this book send a check for $3.95 + $1.50 for shipping. (TX residents add 8.25 % sales tax) to Cookbook Cupboard, P.O. Box 50053, Austin, TX 78763. Send a note asking for this title by name. If you would like a descriptive list of all the fun titles in The Kitchen Crafts Collection and the Layers of Love™ Collection send or fax a note asking for a brochure. Other books you might enjoy are "Cookies in a Jar" (layered cookie mixes), "Gift Mixes" (assorted mixes -11 of which are layered in jars). All the Kitchen Crafts and Layers of Love™ titles are $3.95. There is only one shipping charge of $1.50 per order, not per book.

Layered Soup Mixes in Jars - Introduction

This book is full of original soup mixes for you to layer in pint or quart jars. The soup mixes are great to give as gifts and for fund raisers and bazaars. They are inexpensive to make. Each soup mix recipe specifies which size jar to use for that recipe. There is a complete list of all the recipes in the index on pg. 32.

The recipes in this book give you:
1) - a list of ingredients for the jar.
2) - the order in which to place ingredients in jar.
3) - instructions for you to copy to attach to the jar.

Also included are "Extra Little Gifties". These are mixes or spreads for you to include with the soup mixes. The "Extra Little Gifties" are things the recipient could enjoy with the soup. Most soup meals include salad and bread. The "Extra Little Gifties" are Cajun Cornbread Seasoning Mix, Onion Dill Bread Mix, Crunchy Croutons, Cracker Snackers, Salad Crumble, Salad Sprinkle, Herb Butter, Spicy Spread, Tomato Soup Seasoning, and Parmesan Herb Seasoning that can be used for Monkey Bread, Crescent Rolls or Salad Dressing.

Make Some Soup Mixes For Your Kitchen

Keep these handy mixes on hand in your own kitchen. For personal use it is simpler to put the ingredients into a large heavy duty plastic zipper bag instead of a jar. Grab a bag of soup mix when you don't know what to cook.

How Long Are The Mixes Fresh?

The soup mixes that are 100% beans (or pasta) and seasonings will last 1 year. The other soup mixes will stay fresh 4 months. Put an expiration date on your jars - "Please enjoy this soup by March 1, 2000" for example.

Let Them Eat Soup!

Have a soup party (or a soup bridge game or a soup Bunko party). Serve 2 or 3 soups, salad and crusty bread. Give each guest a decorated jar of soup mix to take home.

What Kind Of Jars To Use

These recipes call for either a wide mouth pint size or wide mouth quart size canning jar. They are sold in cases of 12 jars. Get at grocery stores, hardware stores and discount stores.

Regular (not wide mouth) jars will also work as will pint and quart mayonnaise jars. If you are using food jars (such as spaghetti sauce jars), be very sure they are a true pint (16 oz.) and a true quart (32 oz.). Food companies are making jars smaller each year.

The wide mouth jars are easiest to work with because it is easier to get your fingers into these jars for pressing and leveling the ingredients.

Look For Other Fun Jars

Import stores have several alternative jars. There is a squarish glass jar with a clamp down lid. It comes in 1 liter and 500 milliliter size. Use the 1 liter in place of the quart jar in these recipes and use the 500 milliliter (which is a half liter) for the pint recipes (you will have to add a very few more ingredients to completely fill these jars but that won't effect the recipe).

If you find a jar you like but it isn't marked 1 liter or 500 milliliters, buy one and take it home and fill it with water or rice and measure how much it holds.

The pint recipes need a jar that will hold 2 cups - the quart recipes need a jar that will hold 4 cups.

The jars from the import stores are more expensive than canning jars. They cost $3.00 to $6.00 each as opposed to 65¢ to 75¢ for the canning jars, so think about the budget for your gifts.

Tips

Place the empty jar into a very large mixing bowl before filling with beans - the bowl will catch spillover.

Some of the mixes call for seasonings that are added loose - in their own layer. Some of the mixes require the seasonings to be placed in a thin sandwich bag first. When using these seasoning bags, be sure to flatten the bag so it is visible from all sides of the jar.

When the seasonings have to be in a bag it is because the seasoning packet must be removed before making the recipe. You couldn't remove the seasonings if they were placed loose in the jar.

How To Decorate The Jars

1) Cover lid with a circle of fabric. Hold in place with a rubber band and tie on a ribbon or raffia bow. You can place a small amount of fiberfill padding under the fabric for a "puffy" look.
2) Tape flat lid onto the jar and place a circle of fabric over that. Screw on the ring to hold fabric in place.
3) Fabric is available to match any theme. Go to a fabric store and be amazed at the amount of styles - chicken fabric for chicken soups, every holiday fabric, dice fabrics for Bunko prizes, playing card fabrics for bridge prizes, school fabric for teacher gifts - more.
4) Cross stitch or appliqué the fabric for the lid.
5) Use wrapping paper or brown paper sack instead of fabric (rubber stamp on the brown paper sack).
6) Attach a wooden spoon to the jar.
7) Try to find the 2" bottles of Tabasco® - attach to jar.

Soup Mixes in Gift Baskets

1) Place soup mix into a balsa wood "crate" type box from the craft store. Place excelsior (craft store) in box first and then lay in the soup mix. Tie it up with colorful printed ribbon and tie on a bow.
2) Place soup mix in a basket with a wooden spoon, a package of breadsticks and some "Extra Little Gifties".

3. For a wedding shower, place several jars of soup mix on excelsior in a large soup pot. Add wooden spoons and tie all up with cellophane and a big bow. (We have several good cookbooks for brides - see copyright page for information on getting a brochure.)

How To Write The Instructions

1) Copy the instructions onto a recipe card and tie on to the jar or tape on the front of the jar.
2) Type the instructions into your computer and print out. Add graphics or use a color printer (or use colored paper in your printer).
3) Rubber stamp the recipe card with fun designs.
4) Add stickers to the recipe card.

Ingredient Info

Beans

All the beans called for in these recipes are dried They are found in their own section of the store and are sold in 1 and 2 pound bags (or they are sold in bulk in health food and bulk food stores). A 1 pound bag contains about 2 cups of beans.

Bouillon Granules

This is chicken or beef broth flavoring. Don't buy bouillon cubes - be sure you are buying granules. They are sold in small containers in soup section of the store.

Dried Onion, Dried Garlic, Dried Parsley Flakes

Sold in small bottles in the spice section of the store or in large containers at the wholesale clubs.

Powdered Coffee Creamer

Like Coffee-Mate® and Cremora®. Be sure to get the unflavored kind. Don't use the low fat version. These are available in very large containers (usually a generic or store brand) at most stores and warehouse clubs.

Imitation Bacon Bits

Sold in small bottles in the salad dressing section of the store. Don't use the ones called "real" bacon bits. They won't last for prolonged storage.

Grated Parmesan

Use the green can. Don't grate fresh Parmesan or buy fresh grated. It won't last for storage.

Knorr® products

This is a line of soups and pasta sauces that is sold nationwide. The cheese sauce and the pesto sauce called for in this book are found in the pasta section of the store with the jars of ready made pasta sauce and pasta sauce packets.

Chicken or Pork Gravy Packets

These are little packets sold with the chili seasoning packets and taco sauce packets.

Including A Can Of Ham Or Chicken With The Mix

Several of the recipes in this book require you to include a 5 oz. can of ham or chicken with the soup mix.

This is the size of a regular tuna can. Cans of ham and chicken are found in the tuna section of the store. Don't get a larger size than 5 oz. because it won't fit on the jar.

Tape the can to the top of the jar using 2 lengths of clear tape. Cut a larger than normal circle of fabric so it will cover the can as well as the top part of the jar.

A fun thing for you or your children to do is to relabel the can. Use your computer to make a cute label or rubber stamp it or have your children draw it freehand. Remove the label that came on the can and use it for a pattern for the size of the label you are making. Tape on your label. It should say something like "To Nana - Special Chicken for Soup - Love from Susie and Michael" or "Pat's Ham for Navy Bean and Ham Soup".

Preparing The Beans For Cooking

The bean soup recipes in this book have a shortcut way for the recipient to soak the hard dry beans. The instructions are to cover the beans with water and microwave 15 minutes. If you know the recipient doesn't have a microwave you can change the preparation of the beans to one of these 2 methods.

In the directions you write you will substitute one of the paragraphs below in place of the paragraph about microwaving the beans.

Method A: Rinse beans (or peas). Place in a large pan. Cover with water to 3" above top of beans. Set aside to soak overnight or all day. After soaking drain off water and rinse beans well.

Method B: Rinse beans (or peas). Place in a large pan. Cover with water to 2" above top of beans. Bring to a boil. Reduce heat. Simmer 2 minutes. Remove from heat. Cover. Let stand 1 hour. Drain and rinse.

At this point the beans will be ready to make into soup.

Rainbow Bean Soup Mix in a Quart Jar

Ingredients for Jar

generous 3/4 cup each of the following beans:
- dried red beans
- dried Great Northern beans
- dried split peas
- dried lentils*
- dried black beans

Seasonings: Mix and place in a thin zipper sandwich bag.

2 Tb. dried minced onion
2 Tb. beef bouillon granules (sold in soup section)
2 Tb. dried parsley flakes
2 tsp. dried basil
2 tsp. powdered lemonade mix with sugar
1 1/2 tsp. chili powder
1 tsp. garlic powder
1 tsp. pepper
1 tsp. dried oregano

* Look for red lentils or yellow split peas for a real rainbow of colors in this mix. Look in large supermarkets, bulk food or health food stores.
If you can't find, use regular brown lentils or pick a colorful dried bean of your choice for this layer.

Optional: Top jar with a 5 oz. can of ham. (See pg. 7.) If you do this, change the instructions on pg. 9 to say "Add 8 cups water, <u>ham</u> and . . . ".

Size of Jar: Quart

Place ingredients in jar in this order:

1. Place each type of beans in jar in the order listed above.
2. Top with seasoning bag. Gently flatten bag so it can be seen from all sides of jar.
3. Put lid on jar.
4. Decorate jar (see pg. 5).
5. Attach recipe on pg. 9 to the jar.

This recipe continued from pg. 8.

Rainbow Bean Soup

1. Remove seasoning packet. Set aside.
2. Rinse beans. Place beans in large microsafe dish. Cover with water 1" to 2" over top of beans. Cover dish loosely with plastic wrap. Microwave on high 15 minutes, rotating after 7 minutes. Drain and rinse beans very well.
3. Place beans in very large pan.
4. Add 8 cups water and 1 (28 oz.) can crushed tomatoes and seasonings from packet.
5. Cover, bring to a boil. Lower heat, cover pan and simmer 1 1/2 hours or until beans are tender. Stir occasionally.

Makes 12 cups soup.

Extra Little Giftie

Cajun Cornbread Seasoning Mix

1/4 cup Hungarian paprika
2 Tb. dried thyme leaves
1 Tb. dried oregano leaves
1 Tb. onion powder
2 tsp. cayenne pepper
2 tsp. garlic powder
3/4 tsp. pepper
1 tsp. sugar

1. Place ingredients in small bowl - blend with whisk.
2. Put into a baby food jar or spice jar.
3. Label this "Cajun Cornbread Seasoning".
4. Give with these instructions: "Cajun Cornbread Seasoning Mix - Add 1 to 1 1/2 Tb. seasoning to a small batch of cornbread."

Navy Bean and Ham Soup Mix in a Pint Jar

Ingredients for Jar

2 cups dried navy beans
1 (5 oz.) can ham

Seasonings: Mix and place in a thin zipper sandwich bag.

1/2 of a (0.87 oz.) packet pork gravy mix
(save other half for another jar of soup mix)
1/2 of a (1.4 oz) box Knorr® Vegetable Soup Mix
(save other half for another jar of soup mix)
1/4 cup imitation bacon bits
1 Tb. brown sugar
1 tsp. dried oregano
1 tsp. dried basil
1/2 tsp. nutmeg
1/4 tsp. pepper

Size of Jar: Pint

Place ingredients in jar in this order:

1. Place seasoning packet in jar first. Gently flatten bag so it is visible from all sides of jar.
2. Fill jar with beans. Place lid on jar.
3. Attach can of ham to top of jar (see pg. 7).
4. Decorate jar (see pg. 5).
5. Attach recipe below to the jar.

Navy Bean and Ham Soup

1. Rinse beans. Place beans in large microsafe dish. Cover with water 1" to 2" over top of beans. Cover dish loosely with plastic wrap. Microwave on high 15 minutes, rotating after 7 minutes. Drain and rinse beans.
2. Place beans, ham, and seasonings from packet in medium pan. Add 6 cups water. Bring to a boil. Lower heat, cover and simmer 1 1/2 hours. Stir occasionally.

Makes 5 cups soup.

Chicken Noodle Soup Mix in a Pint Jar

Ingredients for Jar

Seasonings: Mix in a small bowl.

1 Tb. dried minced onion
1 Tb. chicken bouillon granules (sold in soup section)
1 tsp. celery powder
1/2 tsp. pepper

2 cups wide egg noodles

1 (5 oz.) can chicken to attach to jar.

Size of Jar: Pint

Place ingredients in jar in this order:

1. Place seasonings in jar first. Seasonings are placed in jar loose. Press seasonings down firmly.
2. Fill jar with noodles.
3. Put lid on jar.
4. Attach can of chicken to top of jar (see pg. 7).
5. Attach recipe below to jar.

Chicken Noodle Soup

1. Bring 5 cups of water to a boil in a medium pan.
2. Add soup mix and chicken. Break up chicken meat well with a fork.
3. Bring to a boil, lower heat and simmer uncovered 12 - 15 minutes or until noodles are tender.

Makes 4 to 5 cups soup.

White Bean Chowder Mix in a Quart Jar

Ingredients for Jar

2 cups dried Great Northern beans
2 cups Hungry Jack® instant potato flakes in a thin zipper bag

Seasonings: Mix and place in a thin zipper sandwich bag.
1/3 cup imitation bacon bits
1/3 cup dried minced onion
2 Tb. chicken bouillon granules (sold in soup section)
1 tsp. pepper
1 tsp. sage
1/2 tsp. celery powder

Size of Jar: Quart

Place ingredients in jar in this order:

1. Place beans in jar first.
2. Place seasoning packet in jar next. Gently flatten bag so it is visible from all sides of jar.
3 Place bag of potato flakes in next.
4. Place jar on lid.
5. Decorate jar (see pg. 5).
6. Attach recipe on pg. 13 to the jar.

Recipe continued on pg. 13.

This recipe continued from pg. 12.

White Bean Chowder

1. Remove bag of potato flakes. Set aside.
2. Remove seasoning packet. Set aside.
3. Rinse beans. Place beans in large microsafe dish. Cover with water 1" to 2" over top of beans. Cover dish loosely with plastic wrap. Microwave on high 15 minutes, rotating after 7 minutes. Drain and rinse beans well.
4. Place beans in large soup pot.
5. Add 8 cups water and 1 (14 oz.) can diced or crushed tomatoes.
6. Add seasonings from packet. Stir well.
7. Bring to a boil. Reduce heat, cover and simmer 1 hour and 45 minutes.
8. Stir in potato flakes. Turn off heat. Cover and let stand 5 minutes. Serve immediately. If not serving immediately, wait until ready to serve to add the potato flakes.

Makes 9 cups soup.

Extra Little Giftie

Salad Crumble

1 (3 oz.) pkg. Ramen noodle soup mix
1 (2.6 oz) jar sesame seeds (spice section of store)
2/3 cup chopped cashews

1. Remove flavor packet from soup - reserve for another use.
2. Break noodles - place in shallow pan with sesame seeds.
3. Bake at 350° for 3 to 5 minutes, stirring occasionally.
4. Cool and mix with cashews.
5. Put 1/3 cup mix each into a tiny container or a zipper sandwich bag (tie it into a corner of the bag). This recipe makes 6 (1/3 cup) containers.
6. Give a container as a little extra gift.
7. Include instructions that say "Sprinkle Salad Crumble over a tossed green salad."

Black-Eyed Pea Soup Mix in a Pint Jar

Ingredients for Jar

1 3/4 cup dried black eyed peas

Seasonings: Mix and place in thin zipper sandwich bag.

1/4 cup dried minced onion
3 Tb. chicken bouillon granules (sold in soup section)
1 Tb. dried parsley flakes
1 1/2 tsp. sugar
1 tsp. dried minced garlic
1/2 tsp. chili powder
1/2 tsp. onion powder
1/4 tsp. pepper
1/4 tsp. garlic powder

Optional: This recipe is also good with a 5 oz. can of ham added. See pg. 7 for how to attach it to jar.
If you add ham change instruction #4 on pg. 15 to say "Add 6 cups water, <u>ham</u> and . . . . ."

Size of Jar: Pint

Place ingredients in jar in this order:

1. Place 1 cup of the peas into jar first.
2. Place seasoning bag in jar next. Gently flatten bag so it is visible from all sides of jar.
3. Fill jar with remaining peas.
4. Put lid on jar.
5. If including can of ham attach it to jar (see pg. 7).
6. Decorate jar (see pg. 5).
7. Attach recipe on pg. 15 to the jar.

Recipe continued on pg. 15.

This recipe continued from pg. 14.

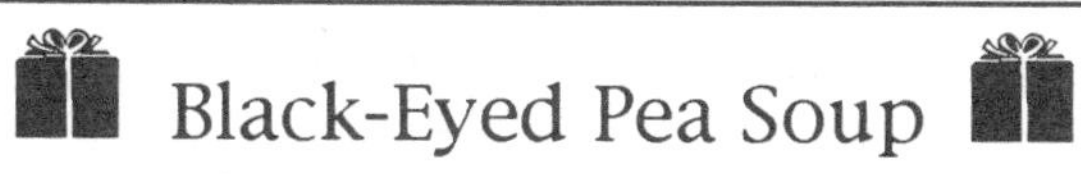

Black-Eyed Pea Soup

1. Empty jar of soup mix into a colander. Remove seasoning packet and set aside.
2. Rinse peas. Place peas in large microsafe dish. Cover with water 1" to 2" over top of peas. Cover dish loosely with plastic wrap. Microwave on high 15 minutes, rotating after 7 minutes. Drain and rinse peas well.
3. Place peas in large pan.
4. Add 6 cups water and 1 (14 oz.) can diced or crushed tomatoes (can use Rotel® diced tomatoes and green chilies).
5. Add seasonings from packet. Stir well.
6. Bring to a boil. Lower heat, cover and simmer 1 1/2 hours or until peas are tender, stirring occasionally.

Makes 6 cups soup.

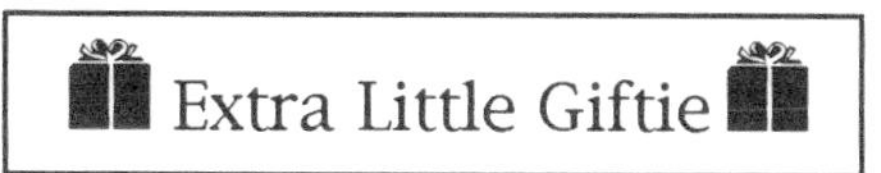

Extra Little Giftie

Parmesan Herb Monkey Bread Seasoning

1. Make a packet of the Parmesan Herb Seasoning on pg. 17.
2. Give that packet with the instructions below:

Parmesan Herb Monkey Bread

1 (8 count) can refrigerated biscuits, unbaked
1 packet seasoning mix
1/2 stick margarine, melted

1. Cut biscuits into quarters and place in large bowl.
2. Add seasoning mix to melted butter and stir well.
3. Pour butter over biscuits and toss to coat very well.
4. Place biscuit pieces in medium loaf pan (4 1/2" x 8 1/4") and bake at 350° for 20 minutes.

Serve immediately.

Wild Rice and Barley Soup Mix in a Pint Jar

Ingredients for Jar

1/2 cup barley (sold in soup section of store)
1/3 cup imitation bacon bits

Seasonings: Mix in small bowl.

1 Tb. brown sugar
1 tsp. dried basil
1 tsp. dried oregano
1/2 tsp. pepper
1/2 tsp. dried minced garlic
1/2 tsp. celery powder

1/4 cup beef bouillon granules (sold in soup section)

1/2 cup wild rice (Reese® brand wild rice comes in a 4 oz. pkg. which is 1/2 cup). You want 100% wild rice, not a blend of wild and white rice.

1/2 cup dried minced onion

Size of Jar: Pint

Place ingredients in jar in this order:

1. Place barley in jar first.
2. Add bacon bits. Spread out evenly.
3. Add seasonings (these are added loose, not in a baggie). Spread out and press flat to edges of jar.
4. Add beef bouillon granules next. Spread out evenly to edges of jar. Press down firmly.
5. Add wild rice
6. Add onion.
7. Put lid on jar.
8. Decorate jar (see pg. 5).
9. Attach recipe on pg. 17 to the jar.

Recipe continued on pg. 17.

This recipe continued from pg. 16.

Wild Rice and Barley Soup 

1. Empty jar of soup mix into a medium pan.
2. Add 7 cups water. Bring to a boil.
3. Cover, lower heat to a simmer.
   Simmer covered 1 hour.

This recipe is also good with a can of sliced mushrooms added. They can be added at the beginning of cooking or stirred in at the end.

Makes 6 cups soup.

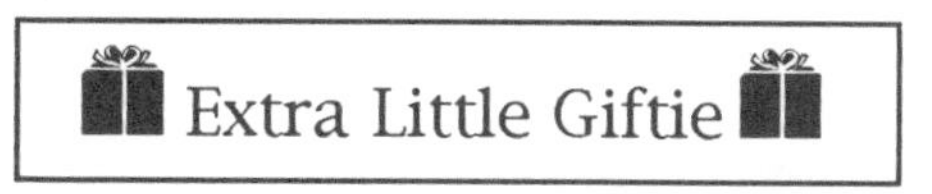

Parmesan Herb Seasoning Mix

3 Tb. Kraft® grated Parmesan/Romano cheese (green can)
1 Tb. dried parsley flakes
1 tsp. dried minced onion
1 tsp. sugar
1/4 tsp. dried oregano
1/4 tsp. dried basil
1/4 tsp. dried thyme
1/4 tsp. garlic powder
1/8 tsp. coarse ground pepper

1. Place ingredients in small bowl and blend with whisk.
2. Place mix into 1 small thin sandwich bag. Tie mix into corner of bag with a twist-tie or ribbon.
3. Copy and attach the instructions below.

Parmesan Herb Crescent Rolls

1. Open a can of refrigerated crescent rolls - unroll dough.
2. Sprinkle dough evenly with seasoning from packet before shaping into crescents.
   Bake as directed on crescent roll package.

Tortilla Soup Mix in a Quart Jar

Ingredients for Jar

1 cup converted long grain rice (Uncle Ben's® is good)
2 to 2 1/2 cups crushed tortilla chips
1 (5 oz.) can chicken

Seasonings: Mix the following and place in a thin zipper sandwich bag.

2 Tb. chicken bouillon granules (sold in soup section)
2 tsp. lemonade powder with sugar
1 tsp. lemon pepper
1 tsp. dried cilantro leaves (McCormick®)
1/2 tsp. garlic powder
1/2 tsp. ground cumin
1/2 tsp. salt
1/4 cup dried minced onion

Size of Jar: Quart

Place ingredients in jar in this order:

1. Place rice in jar first.
2. Place seasoning packet into jar next. Gently flatten bag so it is visible from all sides of jar.
3. Fill jar with tortilla chips.
4. Put lid on jar.
5. Attach can of chicken to top of jar (see pg. 7).
6. Decorate jar (see pg. 5).
7. Attach recipe from pg. 19 to jar.

Recipe continued on pg. 19.

This recipe continued from pg. 18.

Tortilla Soup

1. Carefully empty tortilla chips from jar into a dish. Set aside.
2. Remove seasoning packet. Set aside.
3. Place rice in large pan. Add 10 cups water and 1 (10 oz.) can diced tomatoes and green chilies and seasonings from packet.
4. Bring to a boil. Lower heat, cover and simmer 20 minutes.
5. Add tortilla chips. Cover and simmer 5 more minutes. Serve immediately.

Makes 12 cups soup.

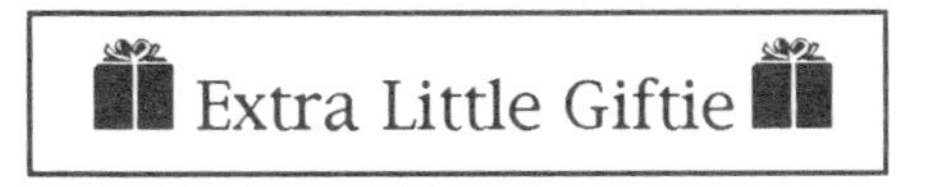

Extra Little Giftie

Parmesan Herb Salad Dressing Mix

1. Make a packet of the Parmesan Herb Seasoning on pg. 17.
2. Give that packet with the instructions below:

Parmesan Herb Salad Dressing

1. Place 1/2 cup good quality olive oil into a jar.
2. Add 1/4 cup cider vinegar.
3. Add seasonings from packet.
4. Place lid on jar and shake until blended.
5. Serve over green salad.

Makes 3/4 cup salad dressing.

Tortellini Soup Mix in a Pint Jar

Ingredients for Jar

Seasonings: Mix in small bowl.

1 (1.5 oz.) packet Knorr® Sun Dried Tomato Pesto sauce
1 Tb. chicken bouillon granules
1 tsp. sugar
1/2 tsp. salt

1 (8 oz.) bag DaVinci® tortellini (Parmesan cheese flavor)

IMPORTANT NOTE: This is a dried tortellini - it is on the store shelf with the regular spaghetti and macaroni. Don't use tortellini from refrigerator case.

Size of Jar: Pint

Place ingredients in jar in this order:

1. Place seasonings in jar first. Level them with your fingers and press in firmly.
2. Place tortellini in jar next.
3. Put lid on jar.
4. Decorate jar (see pg. 5)
5. Attach the recipe below to the jar.

Tortellini Soup

1. Bring 6 cups water to a boil in a large pan.
2. Empty jar of soup mix into boiling water. Stir well.
3. Bring back to a boil. Cover. Lower heat and simmer for 25 minutes.

Makes 5 cups soup.

Black Bean Soup Mix in a Pint Jar

Ingredients for Jar

Seasonings: Mix in small bowl.

2 Tb. dried minced onion
1 (0.87 oz.) packet brown gravy mix
1 (1.25 oz) packet chili seasoning

1/4 cup dried parsley flakes

1 1/2 cups dried black beans (put in a thin sandwich bag)

Size of Jar: Pint

Place ingredients in jar in this order:

1. Place chili mixture in jar first. Press in well.
2. Place parsley flakes in jar next.
3. Put baggie of beans in jar next. Press in well.
4. Put lid on jar.
5. Decorate jar (see pg. 5)
6. Attach recipe below to the jar.

Black Bean Soup

1. Remove bag of beans. Rinse beans. Place beans in large microsafe dish. Cover with water 1" to 2" over top of beans.Cover dish loosely with plastic wrap. Microwave on high 15 minutes, rotating after 7 minutes. Drain and rinse beans very well.
2. Place beans and seasonings in medium pot. Add 5 cups water and 1 (10 oz.) can Rotel® Tomatoes and Green Chilies. Bring to a boil. Lower heat, cover and simmer 1 hour and 45 minutes.

Makes 6 cups soup.

Split Pea Soup Mix in a Pint Jar

Ingredients for Jar

Mix the following 6 ingredients in a medium bowl:

1/2 cup Hungry Jack® instant potato flakes
2 Tb. dried minced onion
1 tsp. chicken bouillon granules (sold in soup section)
1 tsp. powdered lemonade mix with sugar
1/2 tsp. dried minced garlic
1/2 tsp. salt

1 1/2 cups dried split peas

Mix the following in a small bowl:
1 Tb. dried parsley flakes
1 tsp. dried thyme leaves
1/2 tsp. celery powder

Size of Jar: Pint

Place ingredients in jar in this order:

1. Place approximately half the peas in jar.
2. Place half the potato flakes mixture in jar next.
3. Place all the parsley mixture in jar next (and throw in a few peas - 1 Tb. or so). Spread this layer out and press it down hard.
4. Place remaining potato mixture in jar next.
5. Fill jar with remaining peas.
6. Put lid on jar.
7. Decorate jar (see pg. 5).
8. Attach recipe on pg. 23 to the jar.

Recipe continued on pg. 23.

This recipe continued from pg. 22.

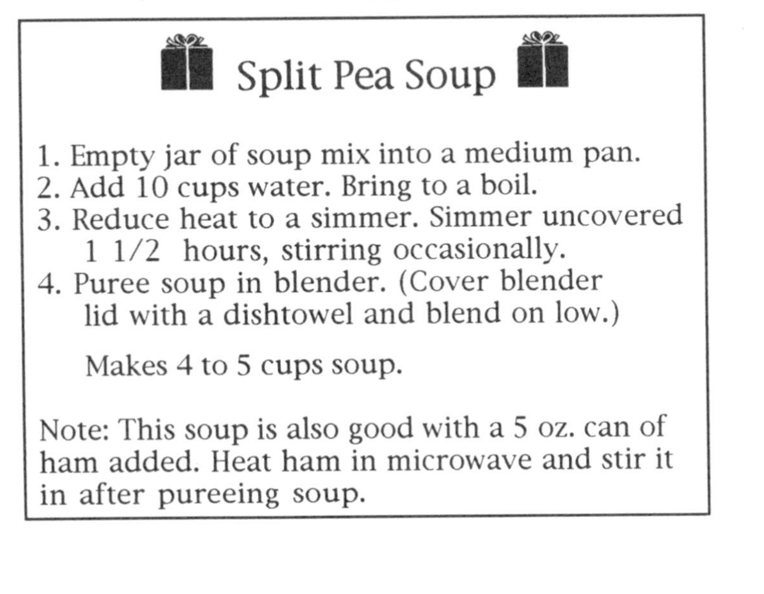

Split Pea Soup

1. Empty jar of soup mix into a medium pan.
2. Add 10 cups water. Bring to a boil.
3. Reduce heat to a simmer. Simmer uncovered 1 1/2 hours, stirring occasionally.
4. Puree soup in blender. (Cover blender lid with a dishtowel and blend on low.)

Makes 4 to 5 cups soup.

Note: This soup is also good with a 5 oz. can of ham added. Heat ham in microwave and stir it in after pureeing soup.

Extra Little Giftie

Cracker Snackers

3/4 cup oil
1 (1 oz.) packet Hidden Valley® Ranch salad dressing mix (original style)
1 Tb. dried dillweed
1 Tb. lemon pepper
1/4 tsp. garlic powder
1/4 tsp. onion powder
1 (11 oz.) package oyster crackers

1. Place all ingredients except crackers in small bowl. Blend well with a whisk.
2. Place crackers in very large pan. Pour oil mixture over crackers and toss well to evenly coat crackers with seasonings.
3. Bake at 250° for 1 hour, stirring every 15 minutes.
4. Divide into 4 or 5 zipper sandwich bags (3/4 cup to 1 cup each) and give as a little extra gift with any of the soup mixes in this book. Give with instructions that say: "Cracker Snackers - Sprinkle on soup or salad or serve as a snack".

Creamy Cheese Soup in a Pint Jar

Ingredients for Jar

Mix in small bowl:
1/2 of a (1.5 oz.) packet Knorr® Four Cheese Sauce Mix
(reserve other half for another jar of soup mix).
1 1/2 tsp. chicken bouillon granules (sold in soup
section of store)
1/4 tsp. pepper

Mix in small bowl:
1/2 of a (1.4 oz.) packet Knorr® Vegetable Soup Mix
(reserve other half for another jar of soup mix)
2 Tb. dried parsley flakes

Mix in small bowl:
1 1/2 cups powdered coffee creamer
2 Tb. cornstarch

Size of Jar: Pint

Place ingredients in jar in this order:

1. Place cheese mixture into jar first.
   Press down firmly.
2. Place vegetable mixture into jar next.
   Press down firmly.
3. Place coffee creamer mixture into jar next.
   Add a little more creamer if necessary to fill jar.
4. Put lid on jar.
5. Decorate jar (see pg. 5)
6. Attach recipe on pg. 25 to the jar.

Recipe continued on pg. 25.

This recipe continued from pg. 24.

Creamy Cheese Soup

1. Empty jar of soup mix into a medium pan. Mix dry ingredients well with a whisk.
2. Add 2 1/2 cups boiling water. Mix well with a whisk.
3. Bring to a boil. Boil 3 to 5 minutes, stirring very often, scraping bottom of pan often.

Makes 3 cups soup.

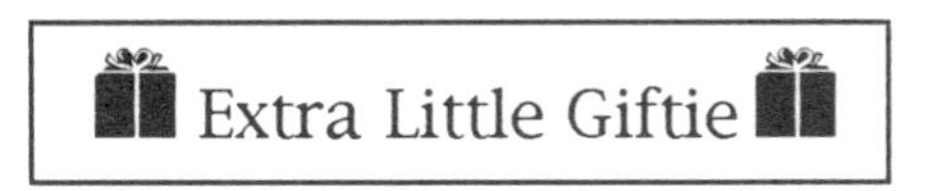

Extra Little Giftie

Onion Dill Bread Mix

2 cups Bisquick®
2 Tb. Lipton Recipes Secrets® Golden Onion Soup Mix
1/2 tsp. coarse black pepper
1 tsp. dried dillweed

1. Place Bisquick® in a zipper sandwich bag.
2. Place remaining 3 ingredients in a thin sandwich bag. Tie ingredients into corner of this bag. Cut off excess bag. Attach spice bag to bag of Bisquick®.
3. This recipe makes one 8" x 3 7/8" mini loaf pan. Buy a package of disposable loaf pans in this size. Give the mix inside the foil pan. That way the recipient will have the exact size pan they need.
4. Copy and attach these instructions: "Onion Dill Bread"
   1. Empty mix and spice packet into a mixing bowl.
   2. Blend with a whisk.
   3. Add 2 eggs and 1/2 cup milk.
   4. Mix until just blended.
   5. Pour batter into 1 well sprayed 8" x 3 7/8" loaf pan.
   6. Bake at 375° for 30 -35 minutes.

Cheesy Potato Soup Mix in a Pint Jar

Ingredients for Jar

1 cup powdered coffee creamer
1/4 cup imitation bacon bits

Seasonings: Mix in small bowl.

1 (1.5 oz.) packet Knorr® Four Cheese Sauce Mix
1 Tb. dried parsley flakes
1 tsp. salt free seasoning blend (Mrs. Dash®, Spike® or a similar blend)
1/2 tsp. dried minced onion
1/4 tsp. pepper

1 cup Hungry Jack® potato flakes

Size of Jar: Pint

Place ingredients in jar in this order:

1. Place creamer in jar first. Push down firmly.
2. Add bacon bits next. Spread them out evenly and push down firmly.
3. Add seasonings mixture next. (These are added loose, not in a baggie.) Press in place firmly.
4. Add potato flakes in two portions. Push each portion in very firmly to make it all fit.
5. Put lid on jar.
6. Decorate jar (see pg. 5)
7. Attach recipe on pg. 27 to the jar.

Note: This soup is also good with a (5 oz.) can of ham. Follow directions on pg. 7 for attaching can to top of jar and decorating jar.

If you include the can of ham change instruction #2 on page 27 to say "Add 3 cups boiling water. Mix well with a whisk. While the soup is standing 5 minutes, heat ham in microwave. Add heated ham to soup. Mix well. Serve immediately."

Recipe continued on pg. 27.

This recipe continued from pg. 26.

Cheesy Potato Soup

1. Empty jar of soup mix into a medium pan.
   Blend dry ingredients together with a whisk.
2. Add 3 cups boiling water. Mix well with a whisk.
   Let stand 5 minutes.

   Makes 3 to 4 cups soup.

Extra Little Giftie

Salad Sprinkle

1. Fill a spice bottle or baby food jar (or something else that holds 1/3 to 1/2 cup) with croutons. (Buy a box of croutons in the salad dressing section of the store or make your own. There is a recipe in this book on pg. 29.)

2. Mix the following seasonings in a small bowl:

   1 Tb. imitation bacon bits
   1 Tb. Parmesan cheese (green can)
   1 Tb. dried parsley flakes
   1 tsp. salt free herb seasoning (Mrs. Dash®
   or Spike® or a similar blend)
   1/4 tsp. pepper
   1/4 tsp. garlic powder

3. Fill jar with this mixture. Shake jar to settle the seasonings all around the croutons. You may need slightly less or slightly more of the seasonings depending on the size of the jar you use.

4. Attach a recipe card with these instructions:
   "Salad Sprinkle. Sprinkle contents of this jar over a large tossed green salad."

Instant Potato Soup Mix in a Pint Jar

Ingredients for Jar

Place first 3 ingredients in a medium bowl. Blend with a whisk.

1 1/2 cups Hungry Jack® instant potato flakes
1 cup powdered coffee creamer
1/2 of a 1 oz. packet chicken gravy mix (reserve other half of gravy packet for another jar of soup mix.)

1 Tb. dried parsley flakes

Seasonings. Mix in a small bowl.

2 Tb. grated Parmesan (green can)
1 tsp. salt free seasoning blend (Mrs. Dash® or Spike® or a similar blend)
1/2 tsp. dried minced onion
1/4 tsp. pepper

Size of Jar: Pint

Place ingredients in jar in this order:

1. Place approx. half the potato flakes mixture into jar.
2. Add parsley flakes next, using your fingers to spread parsley to edges of jar where it can be seen.
3. Place seasonings in jar next, spreading them to edges of jar. Press seasonings into jar firmly with your fingers. (These are added loose, not in a baggie).
4. Top with remaining potato mixture. Press down firmly to make it all fit.
5. Decorate jar (see pg. 5)
6. Attach recipe on pg. 29 to the jar.

Recipe continued on pg. 29.

This recipe continued from pg. 28.

Potato Soup

1. Empty jar of soup mix into a medium pan.
2. Add 4 cups boiling water.
3. Let stand 3 minutes to thicken. Serve immediately.

Makes 5 cups soup.

Crunchy Croutons

8-10 slices white bread (dense texture is best)
1/4 cup margarine or butter
2 Tb. grated Parmesan cheese (green can)
1 tsp. salt free herb seasoning blend (Mrs. Dash® or Spike® or a similar blend)
1/4 tsp. salt

1. Preheat oven to 250° (very low heat).
2. Cut crust from bread and discard. Cut bread into 3/4" cubes (or use mini cookie cutters to cut star shapes or another favorite shape).
3. Melt margarine in large nonstick skillet. Add remaining ingredients and stir to mix.
4. Add croutons and toss gently with a spatula until well coated on both sides.
5. Place croutons on ungreased baking sheet. Bake 20 minutes, turning over after 10 minutes. They will be golden when done.
6. Place on paper towels to cool. Store airtight.
7. Place 1/2 cup croutons in a zipper sandwich bag. You will have enough croutons for 10 -12 bags.
8. Give a bag of croutons with any of the soup mixes in this book. Include an instruction that says "Crunchy Croutons. Float on soup or sprinkle over tossed green salad."

Curly Soup Mix in a Quart Jar

Ingredients for Jar

Mix following 2 ingredients in a small bowl.
2 Tb. dried parsley flakes
1 tsp. pepper

Mix following 3 ingredients in small bowl.
2 Tb. beef bouillon granules (sold in soup section)
1/3 cup dried minced onion
1 tsp. sugar

4 cups tricolor curly rotini pasta spirals (this is approx. a 12 oz. pkg.) - Divide rotini by color.

Size of Jar: Quart

Place ingredients in jar in this order:

1. Place parsley mixture in jar first. Press into jar.
2. Add bouillon mixture next. Press into jar.
3. Fill jar with rotini, one color at a time.
4. Place lid on jar.
5. Decorate jar (see pg. 5).
6. Attach recipe below to jar.

Curly Soup

1. Bring 8 cups of water to a boil in a large pot.
2. Add soup mix and 1 (14 oz.) can crushed or diced tomatoes.
3. Bring back to a boil. Lower heat and simmer uncovered for 12 to 15 minutes until pasta is tender.

Makes 9 cups soup.

Optional: Cut 1 lb. beef stew meat into small pieces, brown well and add at the beginning of making this soup.

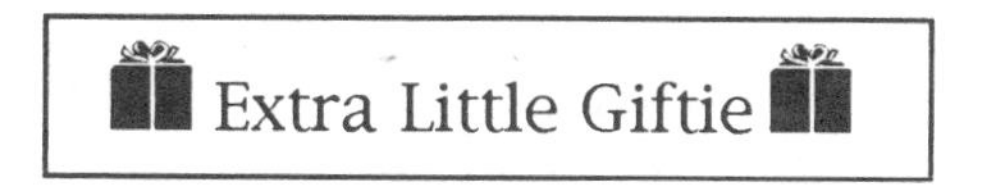

Extra Little Giftie

Tomato Soup Seasoning

1/3 of a (1.4 oz.) Knorr® Vegetable Soup mix
(Reserve the other two portions for 2 other Tomato Soup Seasonings.) Mix soup mix well so when you divide it into thirds you get some of the vegetable flakes and seasonings in each third.

2 Tb. lemonade powder with sugar
2 tsp. chicken bouillon granules
1 tsp. dried minced onion
1/4 tsp. pepper

1. Mix all ingredients in small bowl.
2. Place in thin zipper sandwich bag.
3. Attach recipe below to the jar.

Tomato Soup

1. Into a medium pan, place tomatoes from 1 (28 oz.) can crushed tomatoes, seasonings from seasoning packet and 1 cup water.
2. Bring to a boil.
3. Lower heat, cover and simmer 15 minutes.
4. Serve immediately or puree in blender and reheat for 2 minutes. (Cover blender lid with a dishtowel and blend on low.)

Makes 4 cups soup.

Note from Jackie -

With all these soup mixes you and your friends can say "Soup's On!" any time at all. I got so carried away that I even put 2 more "Extra Little Gifties" on the index page, so be sure and turn the page now for those.

Have fun making up these jars. I hope you enjoy my original soup mixes as much as I did experimenting to develop them.

Herb Butter

1 lb. butter, softened
1 tsp. coarse ground pepper
1/2 tsp. chopped garlic (from jar)
3 Tb. chopped fresh chives.
2 tsp. dried tarragon
2 tsp. dried chervil
1 Tb. dried parsley flakes

1. Mix ingredients in large bowl with electric mixer.
2. Divide among 4 small containers.
3. Give with these instructions: "Herb Butter. Store in refrigerator. Let come to room temperature to serve. Spread on hot bread or rolls."

Spicy Spread

1 (12 oz.) tub soft cream cheese
1 Tb. coarse ground pepper
2 Tb. salt-free herb seasoning, (Spike®, Mrs. Dash®, etc.)

1. Place cream cheese in bowl.
2. Add seasonings. Mix well.
3. Give this entire amount or divide it into 2 parts.
4. Place in suitable containers and give with these instructions: "Spicy Spread. Store in refrigerator. Let come to room temperature to serve. Serve with hot bread, rolls or crackers."

Index